MW01092736

THE GOSPEL

~ OF ~

MARY

~ ~ ~ ~ ~

A Fresh Translation and

Holistic Approach

THE GOSPEL

~ OF ~

MARY

A Fresh Translation and Holistic Approach

by Mark M. Mattison

First Edition

Contents

Acknowledgements

I'd like to express my gratitude to all the women and men of the Grand Rapids Writer's Exchange who have played such an important role in my journey as a writer over the last six years. Their constructive criticism of my writing has been invaluable.

Particular thanks are due to those writers and readers who commented on the entire manuscript: Letitia Robinson, Michelle Griswold, Dianne Black, Shawna R.B. Atteberry, Karen Jacobs, Jessica & Bob Koenig, Isabella Riley, John David Muyskens, Michael W. Grondin, Dan Ballast, and Frances Ogle.

Most of all, I'm deeply grateful to my wife, Rebecca, whose graceful and patient encouragement is a source of inexhaustible spiritual strength.

Introduction

Most Christians are familiar with the traditional Gospels of the New Testament – Matthew, Mark, Luke, and John, the four Gospels unambiguously endorsed by the church and currently included in Bibles everywhere. Our curiosity is entirely understandable, then, when we encounter other ancient Gospels bearing the names of Mary, Thomas, Philip, Truth – most recently discovered in Egypt[1] and translated from original Greek manuscripts into Coptic, a combination of Egyptian and Greek used from about 300 to 1000 CE.[2]

How do these other Gospels relate to the New Testament Gospels, and what do they mean for us today? Predictably, most opinions come down on one of two sides. One side defends the traditional "canon" (standard) of 27 New Testament books (including only four Gospels), arguing that the others are all later books twisting the Gospels and representing a "heretical" deviation from true "orthodox" Christianity. The other side argues that some of these recently discovered texts are in fact earlier than the New Testament Gospels[3] and represent a more pure, spiritual and less rigid, dogmatic version of Christian faith.[4]

A less popular opinion – a middle view between the two extremes – is that these "canonical" and "extracanonical" texts are not necessarily mutually exclusive. Spiritual teachers like the French Orthodox theologian Jean-Yves Leloup and the Episcopalian priest Cynthia Bourgeault argue that these texts are actually *complementary* to the New Testament Gospels.[5] While not always meticulous in their biblical scholarship, these authors nevertheless point out that Gospels like Mary and Thomas can profitably be read alongside the traditional four. That's the position taken here – that these Gospels don't represent a threat to historic Christianity (for better or for worse), but rather a deeper and broader appreciation of what Christianity has to offer.

The specific details of dates and literary dependence continue to be debated, but for our purposes some of those issues can be sidestepped by highlighting broad points of consensus. On the one hand, it's widely agreed that our current canon of Scripture was developed over a long period of time. In his classic textbook of early church history, J.N.D. Kelly writes:

> The first official document which prescribes the twenty-seven books of our New Testament as alone canonical is Athanasius' Easter Letter for the year 367, but the process was not everywhere complete until at least a century and a half later.[6]

The "extracanonical" Gospels in question were written before the church's official list had been finalized. They continued to be copied and circulated for some time afterward, but were eventually lost and only recently rediscovered.[7]

Most of these Gospels (both "canonical" and "extracanonical" by later standards) were originally written sometime between the late first century and the third century, decades after Jesus and his disciples traveled around Galilee and Judea. Often copying and adapting earlier Gospel texts, these various authors preserved both oral and written traditions, many of which date back all the way to Jesus himself. Although these texts are attributed to various apostles and their associates, most scholars believe that no one really knows who originally wrote any of them. Interestingly, even the Gospels of Matthew, Mark, Luke, and John don't actually claim that they were written by Matthew, Mark, Luke, or John, nor did the original manuscripts bear those titles – they were added later on the basis of church tradition.

Different Gospels serve different purposes. The Gospels of Matthew and Luke, for example, form the basis of church organization, whereas the Gospels of John, Mary and Thomas focus more on inner spiritual concerns. All have their place. The canonical Gospels don't claim to have the last word – the four Gospels of the New Testament end with the words, "There are many other things that Jesus did – yet if they were written down in detail, the world itself, I suppose, couldn't hold all the books that would have to be written" (John 21:25, *The Inclusive Bible*).

It is in that spirit that Mary's Gospel is considered here: not as a challenge to Christian faith per se[8] (the author of this Gospel clearly did not see it in that way), but as a Christian challenge to overcome the fear and distractions that keep us bound and drag us down in life, an invitation to follow Jesus and find the spiritual rest that releases us from the domination of the world around us. It's an invitation open to everyone, inside and outside the church, both those who are happy to recite the creeds and those who are so discouraged with institutional religion that they find it difficult to set foot in a church. In the pages that follow we'll consider a few of the treasures to be found in Mary's Gospel and what they can mean for us today.

1
Who Was Mary Magdalene?

Not much is known about Mary Magdalene historically. Inexplicably, the New Testament never mentions her anywhere outside of the Gospels, and even there she's hardly anywhere to be found – until the very end when she seems to be the only person standing by Jesus every step of the way, leaving us to wonder why the role of this most faithful of trusted followers is almost entirely glossed over in the story preceding Jesus' final days in Jerusalem.

All four New Testament Gospels attest that Mary was present when Jesus was crucified,[1] and John even states that she was at the foot of the cross (John 19:25). When Jesus was laid to rest, Mary held vigil outside his tomb (Matt. 27:61). She was the first to discover the empty tomb,[2] the first to see the risen Jesus,[3] and the first to proclaim that he had risen from the dead.[4]

Although she almost seems to come out of nowhere in these Passion accounts, her bond with Jesus obviously runs deeper than that of any other disciple. Thomas doubts him, Judas betrays him, and Peter denies him, but Mary stands by him through thick and thin. She's the last person he sees when he dies and the first person he sees when he rises – as if she's Jesus' closest and most intimate companion.

These Gospel accounts reluctantly provide only the most brief back-story of Mary. Mark and Luke identify her as one of the women who followed him from Galilee.[5] The only other reference to Mary Magdalene prior to this is Luke 8:1-3, where Luke alone provides the detail that Mary, together with others, supported Jesus' ministry out of their personal resources.

Some details about Mary can only be inferred. Unlike other women around Jesus, Mary is not identified as anyone's mother or wife, implying that she was likely unmarried or widowed, probably without children, and probably self-sufficient. Her hometown of Magdala appears to have been a prosperous fishing village on the Sea of Galilee.[6]

Another detail Luke provides is that "seven demons had gone out" from her in Galilee (8:2), a description picked up in the much later text of Mark 16:9. (We'll revisit this curious detail in Chapter Six.) Finally, Luke also writes that when Mary, Joanna, Mary the mother of James, and other women first reported Jesus' resurrection to the other disciples, they didn't believe them.[7]

Probably the most compelling account involving Mary, however, is the detailed narrative of Jesus' post-resurrection appearance to her in John 20. This account, in fact, seems to provide the context for Mary's Gospel, as we'll see in Chapter Five.

> Mary stood weeping beside the tomb. Even as she wept, she stooped to peer inside, and there she saw two angels in dazzling robes. One was seated at the head and the other at the foot of the place where Jesus' body had lain.
>
> They asked her, "Why are you weeping?"
>
> She answered them, "Because they have taken away my Rabbi, and I don't know where they have put the body."
>
> No sooner had she said this than she turned around and caught sight of Jesus standing there, but she didn't know it was Jesus. He asked her, "Why are you weeping? For whom are you looking?"
>
> She supposed it was the gardener so she said, "Please, if you're the one who carried Jesus away, tell me where you've laid the body and I will take it away."
>
> Jesus said to her, "Mary!"
>
> She turned to him and said, "Rabboni!" – which means "Teacher."

Jesus then said, "Don't hold on to me, for I have not yet ascended to Abba God. Rather, go to the sisters and brothers and tell them, 'I'm ascending to my Abba and to your Abba, my God and your God!'"

Mary of Magdala went to the disciples. "I have seen the Teacher!" she announced. Then she reported what the savior had said to her. (John 20:11-18, *The Inclusive Bible*)

Why did Jesus ask Mary not to "hold on to" him – especially given the fact that later in the same chapter he invited Thomas to do just the opposite (John 20:27)? This question has perplexed biblical scholars for years. Jesus' explanation that "I have not yet ascended" seems opaque at best.

Years ago Michael McGehee suggested a plausible solution to the problem. His straightforward suggestion was that the Greek word translated as "for" in 20:17 should really be translated as "since" instead. That small change makes a big difference in the meaning:

[T]he text is more correctly rendered as: "Don't cling to me. Since I have not yet ascended to the Father, go to my brothers and tell them I am ascending to my Father and your Father and my God and your God." In other words, Jesus is stating a matter of fact (i.e., he has not yet gone up to the Father) and not giving an explanation of why Mary should not cling to him.[8]

The contrast between John 20:17 and John 20:27 could hardly be more striking. In the former, Mary longs to touch Jesus, but he urges her to announce his resurrection instead; in the latter, Jesus invites Thomas to touch him, which he apparently doesn't even do. Jesus called his followers to do what they needed most. Mary wanted to touch Jesus, but didn't need to; Thomas didn't want to touch Jesus, but needed to. Mary's faith stands out as the more commendable of the two.

Remarkably, though, after this key story about Mary as "the apostle to the apostles,"[9] Mary seems to disappear from the pages of the New Testament altogether. When Paul describes Jesus' post-resurrection appearances, he says Jesus "was seen by Cephas [i.e. Peter], then the twelve" (1 Cor. 15:5), then "over five hundred sisters and brothers at the same time" (v. 6), then "by James, then by all the apostles, and last of all by me" (vv. 7,8, DFV). Curiously absent from the list is Mary Magdalene.

Silence turned to censure in much later church tradition; the sixth-century Pope Gregory the Great conflated Mary Magdalene with the "sinful woman" who anointed Jesus' feet in Luke 7:36-50.[10] Mary the sponsor of Jesus' ministry and faithful witness to the apostles became Mary the penitent prostitute – a far cry from her historical status as one of Jesus' most trusted followers.

Interestingly, according to Luke, accompanying Jesus during his earthly ministry is a prerequisite for an apostle (Acts 1:22), and according to Paul, having a vision of the risen Jesus is a mark of an apostle.[11] Mary is one of the few who actually meets both of those criteria in the Gospels, and it does appear that she was regarded as an apostle by early Christians.

Whereas the New Testament Gospels describe Mary as a "follower" of Jesus (cf. Mark 15:41), the Gospel of Peter describes her specifically as "a disciple of the Lord" (12:1), and the Gospel of Philip describes her further as Jesus' "companion."[12] The most remarkable passage from Philip's Gospel describes their relationship in the most intimate terms:

> And the companion of the savior is Mary Magdalene. The Lord loved Mary more than the other disciples and kissed her often on her [mouth]. The rest of them saw him loving Mary and said to him, "Why do you love her more than us?" (63:33-64:3).[13]

This survey of Mary Magdalene in the Gospels of Matthew, Mark, Luke, John, Peter, and Philip effectively sets the stage for the Gospel of Mary, which essentially picks up where the others leave off. Mary's encounter with the risen Jesus in the garden, her subsequent encouragement to the disciples (of whom she was one), and the jealousy of other disciples over Jesus' special regard for her form the narrative outline of Mary's Gospel, to which we now turn.

2
Mary's Gospel

The translation that follows is based on the Berlin Codex 8502, page 7, line 1, through page 19, line 5 (BG 8502, *1*, 7:1-19:5).

The Berlin Codex contains the most complete copy of Mary's Gospel discovered so far, even though more than half of it is missing. It's a fifth-century Coptic translation of an earlier Greek text. Two smaller Greek fragments dating to the third century have also been found (see the Appendix for details). All three copies of Mary's Gospel were discovered in Egypt. Scholars widely agree that the original Gospel was probably written in Egypt or Syria in the first half of the second century, which would mean it was written at least as early as the latest books of the New Testament.

This translation is presented in two versions: first, one with standard paragraph breaks, with page and line numbers listed like biblical chapter and verse numbers; and second, for those who don't prefer superscript numerals interrupting the text, an unformatted version which tracks more closely with the Coptic arrangement, which (like other ancient manuscripts) contains neither sentence breaks nor paragraph breaks.

In addition to the fresh translation below, a more literal translation has been included in the Appendix for further study. The translation in the Appendix is being committed to the public domain and may be freely copied and used for any purpose.

Formatted Version

Pages 1 through 6 are missing.

7[1]"Then will matter [2]be destroyed, or not?"

The Savior said, [3]"All natures, all forms, all living beings [4]are interdependent, [5]but they'll all dissolve again into [6]their original state, because the [7]nature of matter dissolves into [8]the original state of its nature. Anyone who has [9]ears to hear should hear!"

[10]Peter said to him, "Since you've [11]explained everything to us, tell us one more thing. [12]What's the sin of the world?"

[13]The Savior said, "Sin doesn't exist in and of itself, [14]but you're the ones who make sin when [15]you act in accordance with the nature of [16]adultery, which is called 'sin.' [17]That's why the Good has come [18]among you, approaching every nature [19]in order to reunite it with [20]its origin."

Then he continued and [21]said, "That's why you get [22]sick and die, because you love **8**[1]what tricks you. Anyone who [2]can understand should understand!

"Matter gives birth to a [3]passion that has no image [4]because it comes from what's contrary to nature. [5]Then confusion arises in [6]the whole body. That's why I told [7]you to be content at heart. [8]If you're discontented, [9]find contentment in the presence of the various images [10]of nature. Anyone who has ears [11]to hear should hear!"

[12]After the Blessed One said these things, he [13]greeted them all and said, [14]"Peace be with you! Acquire my peace. [15]Be careful not to let anyone [16]mislead you by saying, [17]'Look over here!' or 'Look [18]over there!' Because the Authentic Person [19]exists within you. Follow [20]that person! Those who seek will [21]find.

"So go and preach [22]the gospel about the kingdom. Don't **9**[1]lay down any rules beyond what [2]I've given you, nor make a [3]law like the lawgiver, or else [4]you'll be bound by it." [5]After he said these things, he left.

But [6]they grieved and wept bitterly. They [7]said, "How can we go [8]to the Gentiles to preach [9]the gospel about the kingdom of the Authentic [10]Person? If they didn't [11]spare him, why would they [12]spare us?"

Then Mary [13]arose and greeted them all. [14]She said to her brothers and sisters, "Don't weep [15]and grieve or let your hearts be [16]divided, because his grace will be [17]with you all and will protect [18]you. Rather we should [19]praise his greatness because he's [20]prepared us and made us authentic people."

After [21]Mary said these things, she turned their hearts [22]toward the Good and they started [23]to debate the words [24]of the Savior.

10[1]Peter said to Mary, "Sister, [2]we know the Savior loved you [3]more than all other women. [4]Tell us the words of the Savior that you [5]remember – the things which you know [6]that we don't, and which we haven't heard."

[7]In response Mary said, [8]"I'll tell you what's hidden from you." [9]So she started to tell them [10]these things. "I," she said, "I [11]saw the Lord in a vision and I [12]said to him, 'Lord, I saw you [13]in a vision earlier today.'

"In response he [14]said to me, 'You're blessed because you didn't waver [15]at the sight of me. For where the mind [16]is, there lies the treasure.'

"I said [17]to him, 'Lord, now does the one who sees a [18]vision see it by the soul or in [19]the Spirit?'

"In response the Savior [20]said, 'They don't see it by the soul [21]or in the Spirit, but the mind which exists [22]between the two is what [23]sees the vision.' ...

Pages 11 through 14 are missing.

15[1]"And Desire said, [2]'I didn't see you going down, [3]but now I see you're going [4]up. So why are you lying, since you belong to [5]me?'

"In response the soul [6]said, 'I saw you, but you didn't see me [7]or know me. I was [8]to you just a garment, and you didn't recognize me.' [9]After it said these things, it left, rejoicing [10]greatly.

"Again, it came to the [11]third power, which is [12]called 'Ignorance.' It [13]interrogated the soul and said, [14]'Where do you think you're going? In [15]wickedness you're bound. [16]Since you're bound, don't judge!'

"And [17]the soul said, 'Why do you judge [18]me, since I haven't judged? Yes, I was bound, [19]even though I didn't bind anything. They didn't recognize [20]me, but I've recognized that [21]everything will dissolve – both on [22]earth **16**[1]and in heaven.'

"After the soul [2]had overcome the third power, [3]it went up and saw [4]the fourth power, which took [5]seven forms:

The first form [6]is Darkness;

The second, [7]Desire;

The third, [8]Ignorance;

The fourth, Zeal for [9]Death;

The fifth, the Kingdom of the Flesh;

[10]The sixth, the Foolish 'Wisdom' [11]of Flesh;

The seventh, the 'Wisdom' [12]of Anger.

These are the seven [13]powers of Wrath.

"They ask [14]the soul, 'Where do you come from, [15]you murderer, and where do you think you're going, [16]conqueror of space?'

"In response the [17]soul said, 'What binds [18]me has been killed, what surrounds [19]me has been overcome, my desire [20]is gone, and ignorance [21]has died. In a world I was released **17**[1]from a world, and in a [2]type from a heavenly type, [3]and from the chain of forgetfulness which [4]is temporary. From now on [5]I'll obtain the rest of the [6]time of the season in eternity in [7]silence.'"

After Mary said [8]these things, she fell silent because the Savior [9]had spoken with her up to this point.

[10]In response Andrew said [11]to the brothers and sisters, 'Say what you will [12]about what she's said, [13]I for one don't believe that [14]the Savior said such things, because these teachings seem like [15]different ideas."

In response [16]Peter spoke out with [17]the same concerns. He [18]asked them concerning the Savior: "He didn't [19]speak with a woman without our knowledge [20]and not publicly with us, did he?

Will we [21]turn around and all listen [22]to her? Did he prefer her to us?"

18[1]Then Mary wept and said to [2]Peter, "My brother Peter, what are you [3]thinking? Do you really think that I [4]made all this up in my [5]heart, or that I'm lying about the Savior?"

[6]In response Levi said to Peter, [7]"Peter, you've always been [8]angry. Now I see you're [9]debating with this woman just like [10]the adversaries. But if the [11]Savior made her worthy, who are you [12]to reject her? Surely [13]the Savior knows her [14]very well. That's why he loved her more than [15]us.

"Rather we should be ashamed of ourselves, [16]clothe ourselves with authentic humanity, [17]and acquire it for ourselves as he [18]instructed us. We should preach [19]the gospel, not laying down [20]any rules or laws [21]beyond what the Savior has said."

After **19**[1]Levi said these things, they started to [2]go out to teach and preach.

[3]The Gospel
[4]According to
[5]Mary

Unformatted Version

Pages 1 through 6 are missing.

Page 7

1   "Then will matter
2   be destroyed, or not?" The Savior said,
3   "All natures, all forms, all living beings
4   are interdependent,
5   but they'll all dissolve again into
6   their original state, because the
7   nature of matter dissolves into
8   the original state of its nature. Anyone who has
9   ears to hear should hear!"
10 Peter said to him, "Since you've
11 explained everything to us, tell us one more thing.
12 What's the sin of the world?"
13 The Savior said, "Sin doesn't exist in and of itself,
14 but you're the ones who make sin when
15 you act in accordance with the nature of
16 adultery, which is called 'sin.'
17 That's why the Good has come
18 among you, approaching every nature
19 in order to reunite it with
20 its origin." Then he continued and
21 said, "That's why you get
22 sick and die, because you love

Page 8

1   what tricks you. Anyone who
2   can understand should understand! Matter gives birth to a
3   passion that has no image
4   because it comes from what's contrary to nature.
5   Then confusion arises in
6   the whole body. That's why I told
7   you to be content at heart.
8   If you're discontented,
9   find contentment in the presence of the various images
10 of nature. Anyone who has ears
11 to hear should hear!"
12 After the Blessed One said these things, he
13 greeted them all and said,
14 "Peace be with you! Acquire my peace.
15 Be careful not to let anyone
16 mislead you by saying,
17 'Look over here!' or 'Look
18 over there!' Because the Authentic Person
19 exists within you. Follow
20 that person! Those who seek will
21 find. So go and preach
22 the gospel about the kingdom. Don't

Page 9

1 lay down any rules beyond what
2 I've given you, nor make a
3 law like the lawgiver, or else
4 you'll be bound by it."
5 After he said these things, he left. But they
6 grieved and wept bitterly. They
7 said, "How can we go
8 to the Gentiles to preach
9 the gospel about the kingdom of the Authentic
10 Person? If they didn't
11 spare him, why would
12 they spare us?" Then Mary
13 arose and greeted them all.
14 She said to her brothers and sisters, "Don't weep
15 and grieve or let your hearts be
16 divided, because his grace will be
17 with you all and will protect
18 you. Rather we should
19 praise his greatness because he's
20 prepared us and made us authentic people." After
21 Mary said these things, she turned their hearts
22 toward the Good and they started
23 to debate the words
24 of the Savior.

Page 10

1   Peter said to Mary, "Sister,
2   we know the Savior loved you
3   more than all other women.
4   Tell us the words of the Savior that you
5   remember – the things which you know
6   that we don't, and which we haven't heard."
7   In response Mary said,
8   "I'll tell you what's hidden from you."
9   So she started to tell them
10 these things. "I," she said, "I
11 saw the Lord in a vision and I
12 said to him, 'Lord, I saw you
13 in a vision earlier today.' In response he
14 said to me, 'You're blessed because you didn't waver
15 at the sight of me. For where the mind
16 is, there lies the treasure.' I said
17 to him, 'Lord, now does the one who sees a
18 vision see it by the soul or in
19 the Spirit?' In response the Savior
20 said, 'They don't see it by the soul
21 or in the Spirit, but the mind which exists
22 between the two is what
23 sees the vision.' ...

Pages 11 through 14 are missing.

Page 15

1   "And Desire said,
2   'I didn't see you going down,
3   but now I see you're going
4   up. So why are you lying, since you belong to
5   me?' In response the soul
6   said, 'I saw you, but you didn't see me
7   or know me. I was
8   to you just a garment, and you didn't recognize me.'
9   After it said these things, it left, rejoicing
10 greatly. Again, it came to the
11 third power, which is
12 called 'Ignorance.' It
13 interrogated the soul and said,
14 'Where do you think you're going? In
15 wickedness you're bound.
16 Since you're bound, don't judge!' And
17 the soul said, 'Why do you judge
18 me, since I haven't judged? Yes, I was bound,
19 even though I didn't bind anything. They didn't recognize
20 me, but I've recognized that
21 everything will dissolve – both on
22 earth

Page 16

1 and in heaven.' After the soul
2 had overcome the third power,
3 it went up and saw
4 the fourth power, which took
5 seven forms: the first form
6 is Darkness; the second,
7 Desire; the third,
8 Ignorance; the fourth, Zeal for
9 Death; the fifth, the Kingdom of the Flesh;
10 The sixth, the Foolish 'Wisdom'
11 of Flesh; the seventh, the 'Wisdom'
12 of Anger. These are the seven
13 powers of Wrath. They ask
14 the soul, 'Where do you come from,
15 you murderer, and where do you think you're going,
16 conqueror of space?' In response the
17 soul said, 'What binds
18 me has been killed, what surrounds
19 me has been overcome, my desire
20 is gone, and ignorance
21 has died. In a world I was released

Page 17

1 from a world, and in a
2 type from a heavenly type,
3 and from the chain of forgetfulness which
4 is temporary. From now on
5 I'll obtain the rest of the
6 time of the season in eternity in
7 silence.'" After Mary said
8 these things, she fell silent because the Savior
9 had spoken with her up to this point.
10 In response Andrew said
11 to the brothers and sisters, 'Say what you will
12 about what she's said,
13 I for one don't believe that
14 the Savior said such things, because these teachings seem like
15 different ideas." In response
16 Peter spoke out with
17 the same concerns. He
18 asked them concerning the Savior: "He didn't
19 speak with a woman without our knowledge
20 and not publicly with us, did he? Will we
21 turn around and all listen
22 to her? Did he prefer her to us?"

Page 18

1   Then Mary wept and said to
2   Peter, "My brother Peter, what are you
3   thinking? Do you really think that I
4   made all this up in my
5   heart, or that I'm lying about the Savior?"
6   In response Levi said to Peter,
7   "Peter, you've always been
8   angry. Now I see you're
9   debating with this woman just like
10   the adversaries. But if the
11   Savior made her worthy, who are you
12   to reject her? Surely
13   the Savior knows her
14   very well. That's why he loved her more than
15   us. Rather we should be ashamed of ourselves,
16   clothe ourselves with authentic humanity,
17   and acquire it for ourselves as he
18   instructed us. We should preach
19   the gospel, not laying down
20   any rules or laws
21   beyond what the Savior has said." After

Page 19

1   Levi said these things, they started to
2   go out to teach and preach.
3   The Gospel
4   According to
5   Mary

3
An Eternal Perspective (Mary 7:1-8:11)

Unless a more complete copy of Mary's Gospel is discovered, we may never know how it originally began. When the Coptic manuscript picks up at the top of page seven, it does so in the middle of a philosophical question. Although pages seven and eight were not originally the first pages of the Gospel, they nevertheless provide a foundational spiritual insight on which the remainder of the Gospel rests.

That key insight is this: *The spiritual world is more "real" than the physical world.* This paradox is the fundamental truth of the world's great spiritual traditions. It's what the apostle Paul was getting at (and what countless other spiritual teachers have said) when he described our natural existence as one of "sleep." After urging the Romans to love each other, he wrote:

> Do this, knowing that it's already time for you to wake up from your sleep, because now life is closer than when we first trusted. Night is almost over; a new day is dawning. So let's throw off the deeds of darkness and put on the armor of light. Let's live decently, as in daytime, not in carousing and drunkenness, not in promiscuity and lewdness, not in strife and jealousy. But put on the Lord Jesus Christ and don't make any allowance for the flesh and its desires (Rom. 13:11-14, DFV).

This is counterintuitive, to be sure. Especially in the West, we tend to trust only what we can see, hear, taste, touch, and smell. Anything beyond that seems, well – speculative, anyone's best guess. But in actual fact, the physical world around us is far less "real" than the spiritual world which we can't perceive with our physical senses. Everything about physical existence is temporary, in sharp contrast to that which is eternal.

This is not, of course, to discount valid this-worldly concerns; on the contrary, as we'll discuss in Chapter Seven, these spiritual realities speak to very concrete power structures manifest in the here and now. But it is certainly to place our understanding of things into perspective.

The extant part of Mary's Gospel begins with this question: "Then will matter be destroyed, or not?" (7:1,2). Jesus' answer may seem curious at first glance:

> The Savior said, "All natures, all forms, all living beings are interdependent, but they'll all dissolve again into their original state, because the nature of matter dissolves into the original state of its nature. Anyone who has ears to hear should hear!" (7:2-9)

To understand this passage, it is helpful to appreciate its philosophical context. Karen King explains:

> The language in which the question and its answer are framed shows the influence of contemporary philosophical debates over whether matter is preexistent or created. If matter is preexistent, then it is eternal; if it is created, then it is subject to destruction.[1]

King goes on to point out that, in characteristic fashion, Jesus does not directly answer the question;[2] irrespective of whatever is the "original state" of matter, it's destined to dissolve into that original state and so is temporary. Anyone "who has ears to hear" is called to perceive this fundamental truth.

From an eternal perspective, the love of the things of this world is dangerously deceptive (Mary 7:21-8:1). On page seven of Mary's Gospel, Jesus explains that that's why "the Good has come among" us, "approaching every [spiritual] nature in order to reunite it with its origin" (7:17-20). What's temporary will perish, but what's eternal will remain (cf. Heb. 12:27). Mary's Gospel calls us to respond to what's eternal (and therefore to be liberated) rather than to suffer from loving what deceives (and therefore hurts) us (cf. 7:21,22).

This leads to Jesus' statement that "Matter gives birth to a passion that has no image because it comes from what's contrary to nature" (8:2-4). Although Mary's Gospel does teach that the physical world exists on a lower plane of existence, it doesn't teach that the physical world is inherently evil. It's not temporal matter itself that's evil or sinful ("sin doesn't exist in and of itself," 7:13), it's rather what emerges when we as spiritual people "act in accordance with the nature of adultery" (7:15,16), that is, immerse ourselves in worldly desires. In their more free translations, both Jean Yves-Leloup and Lynn Bauman add the words "attachment to" in 8:2 in order to clarify the meaning:

"Attachment to matter
Gives rise to passion against nature" (Leloup)

"Attachment to matter gives birth to passion without an image of itself because it is drawn from that which is contrary to its essence" (Bauman)

The phrase "a passion that has no image" (8:3) may sound unfamiliar to some because it presupposes some understanding of Greek philosophy. Plato taught that eternal ideals are reflected in the physical world by images. "A passion that has no image" would then be something that does not reflect a spiritual reality. The Stoic philosophers taught that the passions of pleasure, desire, distress, and fear are the cause of evil.[3] The passion which "has no image" (8:3) is "contrary to [spiritual] nature" (8:4). "Then confusion arises in the whole body" (8:5,6).

Jesus' next statement is difficult to translate.[4] The word that appears three times in 8:7-9 can be translated in a variety of ways, from "content" at one end of the spectrum (Bauman) to "obedient" at the other (Tuckett).[5] Translators have suggested a number of possibilities:

> "It is for this reason that I told you to find contentment at the level of the heart, and if you are discouraged, take heart" (Bauman)

> "That's why I told you to be courageous.
> If you despair, stand up and gaze ahead" (Barnstone)

> "That is why I said to you, 'Be of good courage,' and if you are discouraged (be) encouraged" (MacRae and Wilson)

> "That is why I said to
> you, be obedient
> and if you are not obedient
> still be obedient" (Tuckett)

Karen King tries awkwardly to combine both "content" and "obedient" at the same time:

> "That is why I told you, 'Become content at heart, while also remaining discontent and disobedient; indeed become contented and agreeable'"

Also awkward but perhaps more accurately, De Boer translates:

> "That is why I said to you,
> 'Be of one heart and be without mixing
> because you are one'"

Finally, perhaps closest to the spirit of the text is Leloup's free translation:

> "this is why I tell you:
> 'Be in harmony ...'

If you are out of balance,
Take inspiration"

In the interests of consistency, I've proposed to use a variation of the word "content" in each case:

"That's why I told you to be content at heart. If you're discontented, find contentment"

But the basic idea is being attuned to spiritual reality. "Content at heart" doesn't mean simply feeling at ease; it indicates being in harmony with divine reality through the organ of spiritual perception, the "heart." The word "heart" doesn't refer to emotions. Rather, as Bourgeault writes, the heart was:

classically regarded in the Near Eastern wisdom traditions as the organ of spiritual perception. Within it are understood to reside increasingly subtle levels and capacities of nonphysical perception, the nous [often translated "mind"] being the most subtle of all. It is sometimes called 'the eye of the heart' – a kind of mystical intertidal zone in which divine spirit and human spirit are completely interpenetrating.[6]

That's precisely how the mystic author of Ephesians[7] described the heart when writing about "having the eyes of your hearts enlightened" (Eph. 1:18, DFV). The "heart" is the seat of spiritual enlightenment (Eccl. 3:11).

Equally difficult to translate is the final phrase in Mary 8:9,10. Where are we to find "contentment" or spiritual harmony? King translates "in the presence of that other image of nature." Leloup translates "from manifestations of your true nature," and Bauman splits the difference: "in the presence of the Image of your true nature." However, as compelling as those translations sound, they don't represent the most natural way to read the Coptic.[8] The text literally has the word "image" twice, which in Coptic implies something more like "each" or "every"[9] image. The phrase I've proposed is "the various images of nature."[10] The idea seems to be to seek spiritual harmony from that which reflects the divine nature. Leloup's commentary is particularly profound at this point:

> In fact, this is an exercise advocated by all the great spiritual traditions. It is essential for anyone who would truly engage in a spiritual path, yet it may take different forms, such as spending time in the company of wise and holy people or visiting special places where their presence is felt; and taking inspiration from the actions and attitudes of those beings who incarnate our own true nature and manifest what is both completely human and fully divine in us – those whose inner truth, beauty, and goodness are the signs of the forgotten God who dwells within us.[11]

"Anyone who has ears to hear should hear!" (Mary 8:10,11)

4
Becoming Authentic (Mary 8:12-9:20)

This part of Mary's Gospel contains by far the greatest number of parallels to the New Testament Gospels.[1] These include, among others, Jesus' exhortation to peace in Mary 8:14,[2] warning about false Messiahs in Mary 8:15-18,[3] and teaching about seeking and finding in Mary 8:20,21.[4] Most importantly, however, Mary 8:14-21 tightly weaves together a number of Gospel traditions to focus with laser-like precision on a second key truth. This key truth revolves around "the Authentic Person" (Mary 8:18).

Here are the principle Marian texts about authentic humanity:

"...the Authentic Person exists within you. Follow that person! Those who seek will find" (Mary 8:18-21)

"...we should praise his greatness because he's prepared us and made us authentic people" (Mary 9:18-20)

"...we should be ashamed of ourselves, clothe ourselves with authentic humanity, and acquire it for ourselves as he instructed us" (Mary 18:15-18)

Whereas I believe these translations are accurate, they're nevertheless interpretations of the original Coptic terms. The public domain translation in the Appendix presents more literal translations:

"...the Son of Humanity exists within you. Follow him! Those who seek him will find him" (Mary 8:18-21)

"...we should praise his greatness because he's prepared us and made us Humans" (Mary 9:18-20)

"...we should be ashamed, clothe ourselves with perfect[5] Humanity, acquire it for ourselves as he instructed us" (Mary 18:15-18)

The term "Son of Humanity" in 8:18 is translated by many (including MacRae and Wilson, Tuckett, and Leloup) as "Son of Man." But in Coptic, as in Greek, there are two words for "man." One means "male" and the other is a generic term which more accurately means "human" because it describes women as well as men. That more generic term is the one used in Mary 8:18, 9:20, and 18:16. In 9:20, at the very least, the word definitely includes Mary Magdalene as well as the male disciples like Andrew, Peter, and Levi. Other translations of Mary 8:18 don't use "the Son of Man" but rather terms like "the child of true Humanity" (King), "the Son of Humanity" (Bauman), "the human child" (Barnstone), and "the Human One" (De Boer). De Boer's translation is both more compelling and, I believe, more accurate, but to draw out the implications even further I propose to use the term "the Authentic Person." Here's why.

First, it's highly unlikely that "Son of Humanity" refers simply to Jesus' human nature as distinct from his divine nature, which is how some later "church fathers" used the term. The scriptural meaning of the term is not entirely obvious, as the phrase clearly had a range of meanings. In Hebrew and Aramaic, it was simply an idiom meaning "human," as in Psalm 8:4 (and it's worth noting that Jesus himself originally spoke in Aramaic, not Greek). However, the term was also used in the prophetic scriptures to denote a prophet, as throughout the book of Ezekiel. Finally, it was used in Jewish apocalyptic texts like the Similitudes of Enoch (1 Enoch 71:17) and the book of Daniel (7:13) to describe a heavenly figure who receives a kingdom. In Daniel 7, the "Son of

Humanity" appears to represent the nation of Israel which is vindicated after suffering intense persecution.[6]

Interestingly, in the Gospels Jesus often describes himself with this term when he talks about his own suffering, death, and vindication.[7] The disciples in Mary's Gospel use it the same way: "How can we go up to the Gentiles to preach the gospel about the kingdom of the Son of Humanity? If they didn't spare him, why would they spare us?" (Mary 9:7-12, public domain version).

So is this curious phrase simply a description of humanity generally, a designation of a true prophet, or a Messianic title? Perhaps those meanings aren't necessarily mutually exclusive; it is certainly possible that these different shades of meaning build upon one another, in which case it could blend nuances from all of the above.

In fact, if Jesus himself personally modeled what an ideal human person should be – an "authentic person," someone who remains true to their nature and all that they were divinely intended to be – and if we are called to "follow" Jesus in this – then it makes perfect sense that "he's prepared us and made us authentic people" (Mary 9:19-20) and that we should "clothe ourselves with authentic humanity, and acquire it for ourselves" (Mary 18:16,17). Like Paul who urged his readers to "put on the Lord Jesus Christ" (cf. Rom. 13:14 above), so Mary's Gospel invites us to grow into the authentic people that we were intended to be, to live up to the image of the "authentic person" who dwells in us.[8]

5
Mary and Jesus (Mary 9:12-10:23)

Ironically, the disciples' response to Jesus' parting words is anything but ideal. Far from being encouraged, they grieve and weep bitterly (Mary 9:6), expressing their anxiety about suffering the same fate that Jesus did on the cross (Mary 9:10,11). They remain paralyzed with fear. Fortunately for the disciples, Mary Magdalene rises to the challenge (Mary 9:13) and picks up right where Jesus left off.

It's worth noting that John's Gospel provides the broader context of Mary's Gospel in more than one way. We've already noted the parallel between Mary 8:14 and John 14:27 where Jesus greeted his disciples with peace (cf. Chapter Four, note 2). Here's the context of that verse in John 14:

> This much have I said to you while still with you;
> but the Paraclete, the Holy Spirit
> whom Abba God will send in my name,
> will instruct you in everything
> and she will remind you of all that I told you.
> Peace I leave with you;
> my peace I give to you;
> but the kind of peace I give you
> is not like the world's peace.
> Don't let your hearts be distressed;
> don't be fearful.
> You've heard me say,
> 'I am going but I will return.'
> If you really loved me,
> you would rejoice because I am going to Abba God,

for Abba is greater than I.
I tell you this now, before it happens,
so that when it happens you will believe.
I won't speak much more with you,
because the ruler of this world,
who has no hold on me,
is at hand" (John 14:25-30, *The Inclusive Bible*)

Jesus' comments about leaving "because the ruler of this world ... has no hold on me" foreshadows the story of the soul in Mary 15:1-17:7, which will be considered in the next chapter. Of more immediate note here is Jesus' exhortation to his disciples to not let their "hearts be distressed" because after his departure "the Paraclete, the Holy Spirit" would be sent in his name to "instruct you in everything and she will remind you of all that I told you."

In Mary 9:12-24, *Mary fulfills the role that Jesus promised of the Holy Spirit in John 14:26.* Here Mary functions as the Paraclete, the Helper who urges the disciples not to let their "hearts be divided" (Mary 9:15,16; cp. John 14:27), who reminds them that Jesus' grace "will be with you all and will protect you." It is in fact Mary who instructs the disciples in everything and reminds them of all that Jesus had told them.

Mary's words "turned their hearts toward the Good and they started to debate the words of the Savior" (Mary 9:21-24). Most other translations use a different word than "debate" in Mary 9:23 (MacRae and Wilson, Tuckett, Bauman, and Leloup use "discuss"), but it is exactly the same word used in 18:9 where Levi rebukes Peter for "debating" with Mary the way the malevolent powers debate with the soul in 15:1-17:7.[1] Though "their hearts" were "turned ... toward the Good," the disciples nevertheless lack unanimity about Jesus' words, leading Peter to ask Mary for more (cf. Chapter Seven for a discussion about Peter and Mary).

Mary responds by narrating a vision of the risen Jesus in Mary 10:10-23. As discussed in Chapter One above, the context for the vision seems to be John 20:11-18. King notes, "the most striking similarity is the narrative context: Both gospels affirm that Mary saw the Lord and gave special revelation to the other disciples."[2]

Mary's conversation with Jesus begins with a discussion about the very nature of visions. Jesus pronounces her blessed "because you didn't waver at the sight of me. For where the mind is, there lies the treasure." This last statement recalls Matthew 6:21: "For where your treasure is, there will your heart be as well" (cf. Luke 12:34), but substitutes "mind" for "heart"[3] and flips the two parts of the saying to emphasize the mind.

The brief exchange that follows in Mary 10:17-22 is difficult to translate and even more difficult to decipher. It begins with Mary's question about how visions are perceived. Perhaps the most straightforward approach is the one taken by Barnstone:

> "'Master, how does one contemplate a vision?
> With soul or spirit?' He answers me, saying,
> 'One sees neither with soul nor with the spirit.
> The mind, which is between the two, sees vision.'"

The first part of the equation is clear enough in its philosophical context. De Boer writes, "Mary thinks in the categories of soul and spirit. In the Stoa the soul is the seat of perception by the senses."[4] To ask whether a vision is perceived by the soul, then, is to ask whether it is perceived through the physical senses. The human spirit, by contrast, is the spiritual part of a person that relates directly to the divine. So the puzzling part of this passage emerges when Jesus presents "mind" as yet another category, *between* the soul and the spirit.

Tuckett writes: "How far we can press the anthropological details here is not certain," asking in a footnote whether it implies "a fourfold division of human beings into body, soul, spirit, and mind?"[5] But given the prevalent threefold division of body, soul, and spirit, it is perhaps more likely that "mind" in Mary's Gospel occupies the place of the human "spirit," in which case the Spirit described in this passage may not be the human spirit at all, but rather the Holy Spirit. Consider the fact that the phrase "in the

Spirit" in Mary 10:21 elsewhere describes the ecstatic experiences of visionaries, as in Revelation 4:2: "Immediately I was in the Spirit! I saw a throne set up in heaven, and someone sitting on the throne" (DFV).

Leloup also concludes that the "Spirit" here is the Holy Spirit,[6] and De Boer notes the same categories in the writings of Philo of Alexandria, suggesting a Jewish framework.[7]

The public domain version of Mary in the Appendix follows the Coptic most closely by using the preposition "in" throughout this passage, but I think the following conveys the sense of it well:

> "I said to him, 'Lord, now does the one who sees a vision see it by the soul or in the Spirit?'
>
> "In response the Savior said, 'They don't see it by the soul or in the Spirit, but the mind which exists between the two is what sees the vision.'"

The point, then, is that Mary's vision was neither something which she physically perceived through her eyes and ears, nor an ecstatic spiritual experience, but rather something that she perceived through her higher spiritual consciousness. Though described here as "mind," it's essentially that "organ of spiritual perception" described by Bourgeault earlier,[8] which is why Bauman uses the word "heart" in this text instead of "mind."[9]

So Mary's vision, in the final analysis, is a testament to her advanced spiritual perception. "You're blessed," Jesus tells her, "because you didn't waver at the sight of me. For where the mind is, there lies the treasure" (Mary 10:14-16).

6
Overcoming the Powers (Mary 15:1-17:9)

After a four-page gap in the manuscript, Mary's Gospel picks up in the middle of a story about an unidentified soul ascending toward its rest and encountering a variety of malicious powers that stand in its way, leveling damning accusations against it. On one level, this ascent of the soul can be read as the journey of the soul toward heaven after death. The seven different "powers of Wrath" in 16:5-13, for example, could "correspond to the astrological spheres that control fate."[1] The narrative could then be understood as describing what the human soul would need to know to get past the malevolent guardians or spiritual gate-keepers to finally get to heaven after death.

Interpreting this passage is difficult, however, partly because the four missing pages in the middle of the Gospel obscure the beginning of the narrative. When the story picks up on page 15, we know that Mary is still sharing a vision with the other disciples, and we know that the vision narrates the journey of a soul past multiple hostile powers. But whose soul? Is it Jesus' soul, going to heaven after his death and/or resurrection? Is it Mary's own soul, visiting heaven and attaining unitive consciousness? Or an account of Mary's ascent with Jesus, or a general story about every soul? Unless other copies of Mary's Gospel come to light to fill in the blanks, we may never know for sure. But there are compelling reasons to interpret Mary's vision in terms of the spiritual challenges faced by every human soul in the present.[2]

For one, it's difficult to read about these seven evil powers and not think about the seven demons which were said to have "gone out" of Mary in Luke 8:2.[3] Just as Mary was released from the grip of the seven demons that terrorized her and kept her bound, so Mary's vision in 15:1-17:7 describes the soul's victory over seven oppressive powers whose ravages we've all experienced to some degree – powers with names like "darkness," "ignorance," "wrath," and so on. These powers are thus described in terms that invite us to confront our own "personal demons," so to speak – demons like addiction, anxiety, and anger. Bourgeault writes:

> This section of the text quickly falls into line as soon as we stop seeing it as a stock "visionary ascent" of the soul after death and start seeing it as a dramatic allegory depicting the confrontation with the false self that must be engaged with here and now in order to attain the state of inner singleness that makes visionary seeing possible.[4]

Similarly, King writes that:

> At another level, the ascent of the soul can also be read as a guide for following a spiritual path that leads from fear and instability of heart, such as that which the disciples evince after the Savior's departure, to the unwavering faith and peace exemplified by Mary. In this scenario, the Powers represent the forces within the soul that it must overcome.[5]

The faithfulness modeled by Mary at the end of her vision supports this approach. After overcoming all the malevolent powers, the soul announces: "From now on I'll obtain the rest of the time of the season in eternity in silence" (17:4-7). The text continues:

> After Mary said these things, she fell silent because the Savior had spoken with her up to this point (17:7-9).

Commentators point out the apparent connection between the soul's final attainment of silence and Mary's own silence.[6] In relating her vision of the soul's ultimate destination, she herself models that very story. Mary speaks as one who has made the journey herself, who has embraced her authentic humanity and attained spiritual harmony. It's not difficult to connect the dots between this apparently mythical description of a soul's ascent, on the one hand, and the path of inner spiritual enlightenment, on the other.

Granted, Mary's Gospel does describe the soul as "going up" toward heaven (15:3,4; cf. 16:3), but that in itself need not require a post-mortem setting. As spiritual teachers have always taught, heaven isn't a place somewhere "up there," but rather a dimension that can be reached now in the spirit. One of the most famous mystical Christian texts, *The Cloud of Unknowing* written by an anonymous author in the fourteenth century, describes it this way:

> For in the realm of the spirit heaven is as near up as it is down, behind as before, to left or to right. The access to heaven is through desire. [Whoever] longs to be there really is there in spirit. The path to heaven is measured by desire and not by miles. For this reason St. Paul says in one of his epistles, "Although our bodies are presently here on earth, our life is in heaven." Other saints have said substantially the same thing but in different ways. ... We need not strain our spirit in all directions to reach heaven, for we dwell there already through love and desire.[7]

In fact, the whole point of *The Cloud of Unknowing* is to encourage faithful souls to embrace contemplative spirituality. Spiritual contemplation is all about seeking the direct presence of the divine in our own lives, here and now, in the welcoming space of intentional silence. Two specific examples, *lectio divina* and centering prayer, will be considered briefly in Chapter Eight.

How can contemplative practices – prayer, meditation, chanting, and so on – help us to overcome the powers that challenge us in our everyday lives? Spiritual teachers like Thomas Keating and Cynthia Bourgeault delve into that question in depth. Simply put, contemplative practices are transformative. Even the very practice of "letting go" in centering prayer conditions us to empty ourselves as Christ emptied himself (cf. Phil. 2:5ff), bringing our hearts into alignment with the divine reality that transforms our very consciousness.

This leads to another dimension of the soul's conflict with the powers that be – the social dimension which stems from the spiritual. If the soul's conflict with the powers is understood only as a post-mortem story of spiritual escape from the world, it's easy to dismiss it as an avoidance of real problems here and now. But the narrative of human conflict which follows in Mary 17:10-19:2 shows that the spiritual journey is intrinsically holistic, not escapist. King writes:

> At one level, the *Gospel of Mary* invites the reader to discern the true character of power as it is exercised in the world. It insists that the ignorance, deceit, false judgment, and the desire to dominate must be opposed by accepting the Savior's teaching and refusing to be complicit in violence and domination.[8]

The world's most profound teachers of the spirituality of nonviolence, including Mahatma Gandhi and Dr. Martin Luther King, Jr., have consistently argued that inner spiritual work isn't a *substitute* for social engagement, but rather a *precondition* for meaningful social engagement.[9] That's exactly what's presented in Mary's Gospel.

As soon as Mary completes her story about the soul's victory over the spiritual powers, she finds herself directly confronted by some of her own colleagues, challenging her in exactly the same way that the powers challenged the soul. This escalation sets the stage for the dramatic conclusion of Mary's Gospel, giving concrete expression to Jesus' and Mary's answer to the problem of the other disciples' fear and bondage. The final pages of the Gospel, in other words, are about breaking the violent cycle of dominating and being dominated in this world.

7
Conflict Over Authority (Mary 10:1-6; 17:10-19:2)

The debate following Mary's profound vision is as fascinating and telling as the vision itself. It couldn't possibly be any more relevant and timely for us today, especially given the current debate about women's role in church leadership.

Andrew is the first to respond. He expresses disbelief "because these teachings seem like different ideas" (Mary 17:14,15). He criticizes the content of Mary's teaching, but not her character. The same cannot be said of his brother Peter, who escalates the conflict with sarcasm and personal attacks (Mary 17:15-22).

At least two other ancient texts preserve the tradition of Peter's antagonism toward Mary. In the Pistis Sophia, we read that:

> Peter stepped forward and said to Jesus, "My master, we cannot endure this woman who gets in our way and does not let any of us speak, though she talks all the time (Pistis Sophia 36).[1]

Later in the same text, Mary says that "I am afraid of Peter, because he threatens me and hates our gender (Pistis Sophia 72)."[2] Finally, in the Gospel of Thomas, Peter complains that "Mary should leave us, for females are not worthy of life" (Saying 114).[3]

That same sexism is on full display in Mary's Gospel. Peter becomes indignant over the possibility that Jesus could have spoken "with a woman without our knowledge and not publicly with us" (Mary 17:19,20), asking "Did he prefer her to us?" (Mary 17:22). When he had initially asked Mary to share Jesus' words,

Peter had said that "the Savior loved you more than all other women" (10:3). Now Peter's complaint reflects the disciples' question in another ancient Gospel: "Why do you love her more than all of us?" (Philip 64:2).[4]

Mary's distressed response to Peter is itself the subject of some disagreement among interpreters. At first blush, Mary's response to Peter may seem to contradict her earlier portrayal as unwavering (10:14) and confident (9:12-20); it was the other disciples who demonstrated their weakness by weeping (9:6,14-16).[5] Is Mary's character now lapsing into the stereotypical picture of a weak woman, overly sensitive to Peter's criticism, leaving it to a man (Levi) to defend her? Or could Mary's response rather illustrate what it means to be a genuinely authentic person?

Arguably, Mary's tears in this narrative differ from the disciples' in a significant way. Their tears expressed fear for themselves; hers, disappointment in those closest to her. Unlike Peter and Andrew, who hide their insecurities behind excuses and bluster, Mary bravely appeals directly to her critics. Rather than shouting back at Peter or becoming defensive, Mary takes the higher road.[6] Peter projects his personal frustrations onto Mary, but Mary knows better than to do that. In her every action, Mary genuinely demonstrates authentic humanity and invites us to follow her example.

Similarly, Levi's defense of Mary need not imply a lack of confidence on Mary's part. We all know by experience that a self-defense is often indistinguishable from "defensiveness." Again, if Mary here had allowed herself to be drawn into a one-on-one argument with Peter, the whole debate could have looked like a personal conflict. Bystanders to an argument can't always tell "who started it," and often both parties look equally at fault. Mary's willingness to trust her colleagues to sort through the issues is a sign of maturity, not indecision.

Finally, and most significantly, the conflict concretely expresses the principles illustrated in Mary's vision. In his response to Peter, Levi first calls him "angry" (Mary 18:8), using the exact same word found in Mary 16:12. There, the final form of the power of Wrath is named as "the 'Wisdom' of Anger." Levi goes on to point out that Peter is "debating with this woman just like the adversaries" (18:9,10). In other words, Peter challenges Mary just like the powers challenged the soul in Mary's vision. Interestingly, this portrayal of Peter as an aggressive adversary is consistent with the early New Testament Gospel tradition of Mark, where Jesus himself (like Levi in Mary's Gospel) calls out Peter for being obstinate, calling him "Satan," which means "Adversary" (Mark 8:33).

Levi concludes his comments by reiterating Jesus' teaching in Mary 18:15-21 (cf. Mary 8:18-9:4). At this point, the Greek manuscript says that "*he* started to go out to teach and preach," but the Coptic says "*they* started to go out to teach and preach." The Gospel doesn't clearly state who "they" were. Was it only Mary and Levi who went out to teach, or did Andrew and Peter join them? Did Levi's words persuade the whole group of disciples, ending the controversy and creating solidarity? Or did the disciples split into factions, with Peter and Andrew organizing a sectarian hierarchy instead of joining Mary and Levi in spreading the liberating teaching of Jesus? Those questions remain unanswered, leaving us to wrestle with them among ourselves today. How will *we* respond to the teachings of Mary?

8
Beginning the Journey

In Chapter Six, we mentioned contemplative spiritual practices as methods of seeking spiritual enlightenment. Clearly many practices are well-known among the world's faiths, but the Christian tradition specifically preserves several traditional methods which are profoundly transformative. These ancient paths place us in a position of spiritual receptivity to the Holy Spirit so that we can be transformed from the inside out. Practitioners of these methods aren't necessarily seeking emotional experiences or miraculous manifestations of the Spirit, as in charismatic worship, but consistently seek the quiet, steady work of the Spirit in reordering our inner being.

Two of these practices in particular have been invaluable to my own spiritual growth: *Lectio divina* and centering prayer. Again, these aren't the *only* practical approaches to spiritual enlightenment, but they are tried and true practices which have made a huge difference in countless lives, including my own.

Lectio Divina

Lectio divina (divine reading) is the ancient Christian tradition of prayerfully engaging the Scriptures more intimately than mere reading or study. Though there are many variations in the practice, it involves four specific steps, known by their Latin names as *lectio, meditatio, oratio,* and *contemplatio.* In English, they're "reading," "meditation," "prayer," and "contemplation." More simply, they can be described as reading, reflecting, responding, and resting.

Before practicing *lectio,* settle your mind, slow your breathing, and open your spiritual time of reflection with a simple prayer to clear your thoughts and focus. Slowly reciting a text like Psalm 46:11a ("Be still, then, and know that I am God"[1]) is another way to focus the mind and prepare for the moment.

When your mind is settled, you're ready for first step, *lectio* (reading). Slowly read aloud a short passage of Scripture – any passage. If you attend a church that uses a lectionary, consider reading a text that will be shared in the liturgy on Sunday morning in preparation for that time of worship. During this reading, savor the words and familiarize yourself with them.

After a short pause, take the second step, *meditatio* (reflecting). Begin by reading the text aloud again. This time, open yourself to the guidance of the Spirit. Listen for a word or phrase in the text that shimmers for you; something that stands out, that invites your specific attention. Perhaps it will be something you've never noticed before. Allow yourself to be led. There's no telling what sort of word or phrase it will be; simply let it come.

Sit with that word or phrase in silence for a few minutes, then take the third step, *oratio* (responding). Read the text aloud a third time. This time, consider what the Spirit may be communicating to you through this word or phrase. What images or thoughts arise from your contemplation of the word or phrase? Feel free to offer prayers in response to this divine communication.

Finally, after a few more minutes, take the fourth step, *contemplatio* (resting). Read the text aloud a final time. Then allow yourself to rest in the Spirit and savor the divine Word taking root in your spirit. After a time of spiritual rest, close in thankful prayer.

Centering Prayer

Another type of contemplative prayer is centering prayer. In many ways it's similar to *lectio divina,* but with important differences. Whereas *lectio* is an active form of prayer, centering prayer is passive. It's very much like the *contemplatio* step of *lectio divina* without the other steps.

Like *lectio divina,* centering prayer cultivates quiet contemplation. Set aside twenty minutes for the practice. Sit comfortably (but not too comfortably – it isn't naptime) and close your eyes. Begin with a brief prayer or other expression of your intention to be available to the Holy Spirit. Then clear your mind – completely – to make room for the Spirit.

In that moment of initial silence, you may be amazed at how active your mind really is. In fact it's easy to slip into a dream state, with images, thoughts, sensations, and a million concerns relentlessly bombarding your conscious mind. When these thoughts emerge, it won't help to chase them away with the complaint that you need to not think; that's like pushing back against a spring, using your own strength against yourself. Rather, let the thoughts come, but gently let them go again, floating past you and away from your consciousness.

The method of centering prayer provides an important tool to help you do that with minimal effort: a sacred word. The sacred word in centering prayer isn't something to focus on in itself, like a chanted mantra. It's precisely the opposite – something to turn your attention away from thoughts and images and back to your intention to empty yourself. You need not chant the word ceaselessly throughout your time of contemplation; silently return to the word whenever you become aware that you're entertaining a thought.

The fourteenth-century author of *The Cloud of Unknowing* describes the sacred word in this way:

> If you want to gather all your desire into one simple word that the mind can easily retain, choose a short word rather than a long one. A one-syllable word such as "God" or "love" is best. But choose one that is meaningful to you. Then fix it in your mind so that it will remain there come what may. This word will be your defense in conflict and in peace. Use it to beat upon the cloud of darkness above you and to subdue all distractions, consigning them to the *cloud of forgetting* beneath you. Should some thought go on annoying you demanding to

know what you are doing, answer with this one word alone. If your mind begins to intellectualize over the meaning and connotations of this little word, remind yourself that its value lies in its simplicity. Do this and I assure you these thoughts will vanish. Why? Because you have refused to develop them with arguing.[2]

The recommended "dose" of centering prayer is twenty minutes twice a day. The practice may not lead to any quantifiable *experience* of divine indwelling, but it will unquestionably bear fruit as the Spirit quietly carries on the work of inner transformation. It quiets the mind, rests the body, and can even lower blood pressure. It's a wonderful answer to the everyday commotion that many of us struggle with, and all it takes is twenty minutes. Embracing spiritual practices such as these enables our souls, like that of Mary, to find rest in the silence of the eternal spiritual reality (Mary 17:5-7).

For Further Reading

Contemplative Outreach at:
http://www.contemplativeoutreach.org/

Cynthia Bourgeault, *Centering Prayer and Inner Awakening* (Cowley Publications), 2004

J. David Muyskens, *Forty Days to a Closer Walk with God: The Practice of Centering Prayer* (Upper Room Books), 2006

J. David Muyskens, *Sacred Breath: 40 Days of Centering Prayer* (Upper Room Books), 2010

Thomas Keating, *Open Mind, Open Heart: The Contemplative Dimension of the Gospel* (Continuum), 2002

Appendix
A Public Domain Version of the Gospel of Mary

The translation of Mary's Gospel presented in this Appendix has been committed to the public domain. It may be freely copied and used, in whole or in part, changed or unchanged, for any purpose.

The text is based on the Berlin Codex 8502, page 7, line 1, through page 19, line 5 (BG 8502, *1,* 7:1-19:5). The Berlin Codex contains the most complete copy of Mary's Gospel discovered so far, even though more than half of it is missing. It's a fifth-century Coptic translation of an earlier Greek text. Dr. Carl Reinhardt purchased it in Cairo in 1896 from an antiquities dealer from Achmim and brought it to Berlin, where it was studied by Egyptologists.[1] However, a number of obstacles (including two world wars) made it impossible to publish a German translation until 1955. An English translation by George W. MacRae and R. McL. Wilson was included at the end of the one-volume translation of *The Nag Hammadi Library* edited by James M. Robinson in 1978.[2] Other translations followed.

In addition to the Coptic manuscript, two smaller Greek fragments also came to light in the twentieth century.[3] Both Greek copies date to the third century, which proves that Mary's Gospel was widely copied in antiquity. By interesting contrast, only one Greek fragment of the New Testament Gospel of Mark can be dated as early as the third century.[4]

All three copies were discovered in Egypt. Scholars widely agree that the original Gospel was probably written in Egypt or Syria in the first half of the second century, which would mean it was written at least as early as the latest books of the New Testament.

What follows is a more literal translation than the one in Chapter Two of this book, and it's been supplemented by textual notes with respect to the state of the Coptic manuscript.

This translation is presented in two versions: first, one with standard paragraph breaks, with page and line numbers listed like biblical chapter and verse numbers; and second, for those who don't prefer superscript numerals interrupting the text, an unformatted version which tracks more closely with the Coptic arrangement, which (like other ancient manuscripts) contains neither sentence breaks nor paragraph breaks. It should also be noted that the line breaks are only approximate, since (1) some words wrap around from the end of one line to the beginning of the next, and (2) the syntax of the English does not always follow the syntax of the Coptic. Consequently, it's not possible to number the lines with exact precision.

Formatted Version

Pages 1 through 6 are missing.

7[1]"Then will matter [2]be destroyed, or not?"

The Savior said, [3]"Every nature, every form, every creature [4]exists in and with each other, [5]but they'll dissolve again into [6]their own roots, because the [7]nature of matter dissolves into [8]its nature alone. Anyone who has [9]ears to hear should hear!"

[10]Peter said to him, "Since you've [11]explained everything to us, tell us one more thing. [12]What's the sin of the world?"

[13]The Savior said, "Sin doesn't exist, [14]but you're the ones who make sin when [15]you act in accordance with the nature of [16]adultery, which is called 'sin.' [17]That's why the Good came [18]among you, up to the things of every nature [19]in order to restore it within [20]its root."

Then he continued and [21]said, "That's why you get [22]sick and die, because you love **8**[1]what tricks you. Anyone who [2]can understand should understand!

"Matter gave birth to a [3]passion that has no image [4]because it comes from what's contrary to nature. [5]Then confusion arises in [6]the whole body. That's why I told [7]you to be content at heart. [8]If you're discontented, [9]find contentment in the presence of the various images [10]of nature. Anyone who has ears [11]to hear should hear!"

[12]When the Blessed One said these things, he [13]greeted them all and said, [14]"Peace be with you! Acquire my peace. [15]Be careful not to let anyone [16]mislead you by saying, [17]'Look over here!' or 'Look [18]over there!' Because the Son of Humanity [19]exists within you. Follow [20]him! Those who seek him will [21]find him.

"Go then and preach [22]the gospel about the kingdom. Don't **9**[1]lay down any rules beyond what [2]I've given you, nor make a [3]law like the lawgiver, lest [4]you be bound by it." [5]When he said these things, he left.

But [6]they grieved and wept bitterly. They [7]said, "How can we go [8]up to the Gentiles to preach [9]the gospel about the kingdom of the Son [10]of Humanity? If they didn't [11]spare him, why would they [12]spare us?"

Then Mary [13]arose and greeted them all. [14]She said to her brothers and sisters, "Don't weep [15]and grieve or let your hearts be [16]divided, because his grace will be [17]with you all and will protect [18]you. Rather we should [19]praise his greatness because he's [20]prepared us and made us Humans."

When [21]Mary said these things, she turned their hearts [22]toward the Good and they started [23]to debate the words [24]of the Savior.

10[1]Peter said to Mary, "Sister, [2]we know the Savior loved you [3]more than all other women. [4]Tell us the words of the Savior that you [5]remember – the things which you know [6]that we don't, and which we haven't heard."

[7]In response Mary said, [8]"I'll tell you what's hidden from you." [9]So she started to tell them [10]these words: "I," she said, "I [11]saw the Lord in a vision and I [12]said to him, 'Lord, I saw you [13]in a vision today.'

"In response he [14]said to me, 'You're blessed because you didn't waver [15]at the sight of me. For where the mind [16]is, there is the treasure.'

"I said [17]to him, 'Lord, now does the one who sees the [18]vision see it in the soul or in [19]the spirit?'

"In response the Savior [20]said, 'They don't see in the soul [21]or in the spirit, but the mind which exists [22]between the two is what [23]sees the vision.' ...

Pages 11 through 14 are missing.

15[1]"And Desire said, [2]'I didn't see you going down, [3]but now I see you're going [4]up. So why are you lying, since you belong to [5]me?'

"In response the soul [6]said, 'I saw you, but you didn't see me [7]or know me. I was [8]to you just a garment, and you didn't recognize me.' [9]When it said these things, it left, rejoicing [10]greatly.

"Again, it came to the [11]third power, which is [12]called 'Ignorance.' It [13]interrogated the soul and said, [14]'Where are you going? In [15]wickedness you're bound. [16]Since you're bound, don't judge!'

"And [17]the soul said, 'Why do you judge [18]me, since I haven't judged? I was bound, [19]even though I haven't bound. They didn't recognize [20]me, but I've recognized that [21]everything will dissolve – both the things of the [22]earth **16**[1]and the things of heaven.'

"When the soul [2]had overcome the third power, [3]it went up and saw [4]the fourth power, which took [5]seven forms:

The first form [6]is Darkness;

The second, [7]Desire;

The third, [8]Ignorance;

The fourth, Zeal for [9]Death;

The fifth, the Kingdom of the Flesh;

[10]The sixth, the Foolish 'Wisdom' [11]of Flesh;

The seventh, the 'Wisdom' [12]of Anger.

These are the seven [13]powers of Wrath.

"They ask [14]the soul, 'Where do you come from, [15]you murderer, and where are you going, [16]conqueror of space?'

"In response the [17]soul said, 'What binds [18]me has been killed, what surrounds [19]me has been overcome, my desire [20]is gone, and ignorance [21]has died. In a world I was released **17**[1]from a world, and in a [2]type from a type which is [3]above, and from the chain of forgetfulness which [4]exists only for a time. From now on [5]I'll receive the rest of the [6]time of the season of the age in [7]silence.'"

When Mary said [8]these things, she fell silent because the Savior [9]had spoken with her up to this point.

[10]In response Andrew said [11]to the brothers and sisters, 'Say what you will [12]about what she's said, [13]I myself don't believe that [14]the Savior said these things, because these teachings seem like [15]different ideas."

In response [16]Peter spoke out with [17]the same concerns. He [18]asked them concerning the Savior: "He didn't [19]speak with a woman without our knowledge [20]and not publicly with us, did he?

Will we [21]turn around and all listen [22]to her? Did he prefer her to us?"

18[1]Then Mary wept and said to [2]Peter, "My brother Peter, what are you [3]thinking? Do you really think that I [4]thought this up by myself in my [5]heart, or that I'm lying about the Savior?"

[6]In response Levi said to Peter, [7]"Peter, you've always been [8]angry. Now I see you [9]debating with this woman like [10]the adversaries. But if the [11]Savior made her worthy, who are you [12]then to reject her? Surely [13]the Savior knows her [14]very well. That's why he loved her more than [15]us.

"Rather we should be ashamed, [16]clothe ourselves with perfect Humanity, [17]acquire it for ourselves as he [18]instructed us, and preach [19]the gospel, not laying down [20]any other rule or other law [21]beyond what the Savior said."

When **19**[1]Levi said these things, they started to [2]go out to teach and to preach.

[3]The Gospel
[4]According to
[5]Mary

Unformatted Version

Pages 1 through 6 are missing.

Page 7

1 "Then will matter
2 be destroyed, or not?" The Savior said,
3 "Every nature, every form, every creature
4 exists in and with each other,
5 but they'll dissolve again into
6 their own roots, because the
7 nature of matter dissolves into
8 its nature alone. Anyone who has
9 ears to hear should hear!"
10 Peter said to him, "Since you've
11 explained everything to us, tell us one more thing.
12 What's the sin of the world?"
13 The Savior said, "Sin doesn't exist,
14 but you're the ones who make sin when
15 you act in accordance with the nature of
16 adultery, which is called 'sin.'
17 That's why the Good came
18 among you, up to the things of every nature
19 in order to restore it within
20 its root." Then he continued and
21 said, "That's why you get
22 sick and die, because you love

Page 8

1 what tricks you. Anyone who
2 can understand should understand! Matter gave birth to a
3 passion that has no image
4 because it comes from what's contrary to nature.
5 Then confusion arises in
6 the whole body. That's why I told
7 you to be content at heart.
8 If you're discontented,
9 find contentment in the presence of the various images
10 of nature. Anyone who has ears
11 to hear should hear!"
12 When the Blessed One said these things, he
13 greeted them all and said,
14 "Peace be with you! Acquire my peace.
15 Be careful not to let anyone
16 mislead you by saying,
17 'Look over here!' or 'Look
18 over there!' Because the Son of Humanity
19 exists within you. Follow
20 him! Those who seek him will
21 find him. "Go then and preach
22 the gospel about the kingdom. Don't

Page 9

1   lay down any rules beyond what
2   I've given you, nor make a
3   law like the lawgiver, lest
4   you be bound by it."
5   When he said these things, he left. But
6   they grieved and wept bitterly. They
7   said, "How can we go
8   up to the Gentiles to preach
9   the gospel about the kingdom of the Son
10 of Humanity? If they didn't
11 spare him, why would they
12 spare us?" Then Mary
13 arose and greeted them all.
14 She said to her brothers and sisters, "Don't weep
15 and grieve or let your hearts be
16 divided, because his grace will be
17 with you all and will protect
18 you. Rather we should
19 praise his greatness because he's
20 prepared us and made us Humans." When
21 Mary said these things, she turned their hearts
22 toward the Good and they started
23 to debate the words
24 of the Savior.

Page 10

1   Peter said to Mary, "Sister,
2   we know the Savior loved you
3   more than all other women.
4   Tell us the words of the Savior that you
5   remember – the things which you know
6   that we don't, and which we haven't heard."
7   In response Mary said,
8   "I'll tell you what's hidden from you."
9   So she started to tell them
10 these words: "I," she said, "I
11 saw the Lord in a vision and I
12 said to him, 'Lord, I saw you
13 in a vision today.' In response he
14 said to me, 'You're blessed because you didn't waver
15 at the sight of me. For where the mind
16 is, there is the treasure.' I said
17 to him, 'Lord, now does the one who sees the
18 vision see it in the soul or in
19 the spirit?' In response the Savior
20 said, 'They don't see in the soul
21 or in the spirit, but the mind which exists
22 between the two is what
23 sees the vision.' …

Pages 11 through 14 are missing.

Page 15

1 "And Desire said,
2 'I didn't see you going down,
3 but now I see you're going
4 up. So why are you lying, since you belong to
5 me?' In response the soul
6 said, 'I saw you, but you didn't see me
7 or know me. I was
8 to you just a garment, and you didn't recognize me.'
9 When it said these things, it left, rejoicing
10 greatly. Again, it came to the
11 third power, which is
12 called 'Ignorance.' It
13 interrogated the soul and said,
14 'Where are you going? In
15 wickedness you're bound.
16 Since you're bound, don't judge!' And
17 the soul said, 'Why do you judge
18 me, since I haven't judged? I was bound,
19 even though I haven't bound. They didn't recognize
20 me, but I've recognized that
21 everything will dissolve – both the things of the
22 earth

Page 16

1   and the things of heaven.' When the soul
2   had overcome the third power,
3   it went up and saw
4   the fourth power, which took
5   seven forms: the first form
6   is Darkness; the second,
7   Desire; the third,
8   Ignorance; the fourth, Zeal for
9   Death; the fifth, the Kingdom of the Flesh;
10 the sixth, the Foolish 'Wisdom'
11 of Flesh; the seventh, the 'Wisdom'
12 of Anger. These are the seven
13 powers of Wrath. They ask
14 the soul, 'Where do you come from,
15 you murderer, and where are you going,
16 conqueror of space?' In response the
17 soul said, 'What binds
18 me has been killed, what surrounds
19 me has been overcome, my desire
20 is gone, and ignorance
21 has died. In a world I was released

Page 17

1   from a world, and in a
2   type from a type which is
3   above, and from the chain of forgetfulness which
4   exists only for a time. From now on
5   I'll receive the rest of the
6   time of the season of the age in
7   silence.'" When Mary said
8   these things, she fell silent because the Savior
9   had spoken with her up to this point.
10 In response Andrew said
11 to the brothers and sisters, 'Say what you will
12 about what she's said,
13 I myself don't believe that
14 the Savior said these things, because these teachings seem like
15 different ideas." In response
16 Peter spoke out with
17 the same concerns. He
18 asked them concerning the Savior: "He didn't
19 speak with a woman without our knowledge
20 and not publicly with us, did he? Will we
21 turn around and all listen
22 to her? Did he prefer her to us?"

Page 18

1   Then Mary wept and said to
2   Peter, "My brother Peter, what are you
3   thinking? Do you really think that I
4   thought this up by myself in my
5   heart, or that I'm lying about the Savior?"
6   In response Levi said to Peter,
7   "Peter, you've always been
8   angry. Now I see you
9   debating with this woman like
10 the adversaries. But if the
11 Savior made her worthy, who are you
12 then to reject her? Surely
13 the Savior knows her
14 very well. That's why he loved her more than
15 us. Rather we should be ashamed,
16 clothe ourselves with perfect Humanity,
17 acquire it for ourselves as he
18 instructed us, and preach
19 the gospel, not laying down
20 any other rule or other law
21 beyond what the Savior said." When

Page 19

1   Levi said these things, they started to
2   go out to teach and to preach.
3   The Gospel
4   According to
5   Mary

Text Notes

7:1,2: *"Then will matter be destroyed, or not?"* The words "matter" and "destroyed" are proposed reconstructions, since the top of page 7 is damaged and several letters are either missing or barely legible.

7:22 – 8:1: *"You love what tricks you. Anyone who ...."* This is a proposed reconstruction since the bottom of page 7 and the top of page 8 are damaged and several letters are either missing or barely legible.

8:2: *"Matter gave birth to."* This is a proposed reconstruction since the manuscript is damaged here and the letters are either missing or barely legible.

8:7-9: *"Be content at heart ... discontented ... find contentment."* Or possibly *"Be obedient ... disobedient ... be obedient."*

8:18; 9:9-10: *"Son of Humanity."* Literally, *"Son of the Human,"* a technical term based on an Aramaic idiom meaning "human."

9:24: *"The Savior."* This is a proposed reconstruction since the bottom of page 9 is damaged and the letters are either missing or barely legible.

9:14; 17:11: *"Brothers and sisters":* Literally, *"brothers."*

16:21: *"A world."* This is a proposed reconstruction since the bottom of page 16 is damaged and the letters are either missing or barely legible.

18:16: *"Perfect Humanity."* Literally, *"the perfect human."*

19:1: *"Levi said these things."* This is a proposed reconstruction since the top of page 19 is damaged and the letters are either missing or barely legible.

Notes

Introduction

[1]Probably not because more Gospels were copied in Egypt than other places, but because the dry climate in Egypt is more conducive to the survival of ancient manuscripts. Cf. Bentley Layton, *Coptic in 20 Lessons: Introduction to Sahidic Coptic With Exercises and Vocabularies* (Peeters), 2007: "Because the survival of early Coptic manuscripts was dictated more by climate than by theological orthodoxy, a very wide selection of apocryphal and heretical works has also survived" (p. 2).

[2]*Ibid.,* p. 1.

[3]Cf. the chronological list on p. 6 of *The Complete Gospels* (HarperSanFrancisco), 1994, ed. by Robert J. Miller.

[4]Cf. the comments of Harold Bloom in Marvin Meyer, *The Gospel of Thomas: The Hidden Sayings of Jesus* (HarperSanFrancisco), 1992, p. 111.

[5]Cf. Cynthia Bourgeault, *The Wisdom Jesus: Transforming Heart and Mind — a New Perspective on Christ and His Message* (Shambhala), 2008, p. 5: "I've been reaffirmed in my sense that Jesus came first and foremost as a teacher of the path of inner transformation. That doesn't take away the Jesus you may be more familiar with — the Son of God, the second person of the Trinity — but it does add a renewed emphasis on paying attention to what he actually taught and seeing how we can begin to walk it authentically from the inside." Jean-Yves Leloup, *The Gospel of Philip: Jesus, Mary*

Magdalene, and the Gnosis of Sacred Union (Inner Traditions), 2004, p. 2: "It is not my intention to set the canonical and the apocryphal Gospels against each other, nor to privilege one over the others. My aim is to read them together: to hold the manifest together with the hidden, the allowed with the forbidden, the conscious with the unconscious." Cf. also Leloup, *The Gospel of Thomas: The Gnostic Wisdom of Jesus* (Inner Traditions), 2005, pp. 4,5.

[6]J.N.D. Kelly, *Early Christian Doctrines* (Harper & Row), 1960, p. 60.

[7]Many of them in the now-famous Nag Hammadi library, a collection of twelve leather-bound codices discovered near Nag Hammadi in Egypt in 1945, just two years before the initial discovery of the Dead Sea Scrolls. However, there are many others, including the Berlin Codex which contains the Coptic translation of Mary's Gospel.

[8]Some argue that Mary's Gospel teaches an ancient Christian "heresy" called "Gnosticism." But scholars are divided on whether Mary's Gospel really is "Gnostic" and even on whether "Gnosticism" is a sufficiently defined category. For a broad sampling of very different conclusions, see Christopher Tuckett, *The Gospel of Mary* (Oxford University Press), 2007, pp. 42-54; Esther De Boer, *Mary Magdalene: Beyond the Myth* (Trinity Press International), 1997, pp. 89-93; Karen L. King, *The Gospel of Mary of Magdala: Jesus and the First Woman Apostle* (Polebridge Press), 2003, pp. 155-190.

Chapter One

[1]Cf. Matt. 27:55,56; Mark 15:40; Luke 23:49.

[2]Cf. Matt. 28:1-7; Mark 16:1-8; Luke 24:1-8; John 20:1.

[3]Cf. Matt. 28:9; John 20:14-17.

4Cf. Matt. 28:8; Luke 24:10; John 20:18.

5Mark 15:40,41; Luke 23:49.

6Cf. De Boer, *op. cit.,* pp. 21-31.

7Luke 24:9-11; cf. Mark 16:11.

8Michael McGehee, "A Less Theological Reading of John 20:17," *Journal of Biblical Literature,* Vol. 105, No. 2 (June 1986), p. 299.

9Cf. Cynthia Bourgeault, *The Meaning of Mary Magdalene: Discovering the Woman at the Heart of Christianity* (Shambhala), 2010, p. 8.

10Additionally, Mary Magdalene was conflated with Mary of Bethany on the basis that John 12:3-8 identifies the woman who anointed Jesus as Mary of Bethany. Some interpreters (including Bourgeault) continue to identify Mary Magdalene as Mary of Bethany for a number of other reasons. The suggestion of Margaret Starbird in *The Woman with the Alabaster Jar: Mary Magdalene and the Holy Grail* (Bear & Company), 1993, that "Magdalene" could have been a nickname (meaning "tower" or "great") instead of a description of Mary's hometown (p. 51) is part of a larger argument intended to explain how Mary of Magdala could also be "of Bethany." But it seems difficult to conflate these two Marys on the basis of the Gospel narratives. Mary Magdalene is specifically said to be from Galilee, not from Bethany, and John's Gospel appears to maintain a clear distinction.

111 Cor. 9:1; 15:8,9.

12Philip 59:9,11; 63:33.

[13]Andrew Phillip Smith, *The Gospel of Philip: Annotated and Explained* (Skylight Paths Publishing), 2005, p. 53.

Chapter Three

[1]King, *op. cit.,* p. 45.

[2]*Ibid.*

[3]*Ibid.,* p. 43.

[4]Cf. Tuckett, *op. cit.,* pp. 146,147.

[5]Other possible meanings include "persuaded," "satisfied," and "agreeable," among others. Cf. Thomas O. Lambdin, *Introduction to Sahidic Coptic* (Mercer University Press), p. 289.

[6]Bourgeault, *Mary Magdalene*, p. 60.

[7]Though the epistle to the Ephesians is traditionally attributed to the apostle Paul, most biblical scholars describe it as "deutero-Pauline," meaning that it was probably not actually written by Paul but rather someone deeply influenced by him. On Ephesians as "the charter of Christian mysticism," see Carl McColman, *The Big Book of Christian Mysticism: The Essential Guide to Contemplative Spirituality* (Hampton Roads Publishing Company, Inc.), 2010, pp. 41-46.

[8]Cf. Tuckett, *op. cit.,* p. 148.

[9]Layton, *op. cit.,* p. 20.

[10]MacRae and Wilson, as well as Tuckett, render the phrase as "in the presence of the different forms of nature." The word translated as "forms" is the same word translated as "image" in 8:3.

[11]Leloup, *Mary Magdalene*, p. 65.

Chapter Four

[1]For detailed discussions of the relationship between Mary's Gospel and the New Testament, cf. King, *op. cit.,* pp. 93-133; Tuckett, *op. cit.,* pp. 55-74.

[2]Cf. Luke 24:36; John 14:27; 20:19,21,26.

[3]Cf. Matt. 24:23-26; Mark 13:21-23; Luke 17:23.

[4]Cf. Matt. 7:7; Luke 11:10.

[5]It's worth noting that the word for "perfect" here is actually a Greek loan word which carries more of a connotation of completeness or wholeness than of moral flawlessness.

[6]Cf. Dan. 7:14 with Dan. 7:18,22,27.

[7]Cf. Mark 8:31; 9:9-12,31; 10:33,45; 14:21; et al.

[8]Cf. also the excellent discussions of this term in Jane Schaberg, *The Resurrection of Mary Magdalene: Legends, Apocrypha, and the Christian Testament* (Continuum), 2004, pp. 360-65. Schaberg also prefers the term "the Human One" as an ideal alternative to "the Son of Man" (p. 361, n. 7). She writes: "I think that in the Christian Testament, and in the Gospel of Mary and elsewhere in "gnostic" materials, Son of Man traditions strain to become expressions of full humanity, inclusive of men and women. ... Modern inclusive translations from Daniel and 1 Enoch on into the Christian and "gnostic" texts challenge this rhetorical custom in the name of alerting us to a possible ideal" (p. 364).

Chapter Five

[1]King does use "debate" in 9:23.

[2]King, *op. cit.*, p. 130. Cf. also Tuckett: "The scene here in the *Gospel of Mary* may then be an elaboration of the account in John's Gospel" (p. 170).

[3]The overlap in meaning between "mind" and "heart" is also apparent in Mary 9:21. There, the Coptic manuscript uses the word "heart" where the Greek uses the word "mind."

[4]De Boer, *op. cit.*, p. 108.

[5]Tuckett, *op. cit.*, p. 173, n. 149.

[6]Leloup, *Mary Magdalene*, pp. 118ff. On the one hand, he describes "a fourfold anthropology" in which "the human being is a composite of body (soma), soul (psyche), mind (nous), and Spirit (Pneuma)," but goes on to write that "Pneuma is not itself a component of the human complex" (p. 120) and identifies it as "the Holy Spirit" (pp. 120,121).

[7]De Boer, *op. cit.*, pp. 109,110. She poignantly asks, "Is it possible that here the Savior is presenting in a way comprehensible to Hellenistic ears the Jewish view that God is transcendent and nevertheless can be known by human beings, at least partially? Also through a vision?" (p. 109).

[8]Cf. Chapter Three.

[9]On the other hand, my colleague Shawna R.B. Atteberry suggests a precedent for a fourfold anthropology in the canonical Gospels' addition of "mind" to the threefold "heart," "soul," and "might" of Deuteronomy 6:5 (cf. Matt. 22:37; Mark 12:30; Luke 10:27). Commenting on Mark 12:30, R.T. France writes that "It is

difficult to differentiate clearly between the force of καρδία [heart], ψυχή [soul] and διάνοια [mind] in the context of Hebrew thought, but the addition of διάνοια (BAGD 187a: 'understanding, intelligence, mind, thought') *may* suggest a deliberate extension of the familiar text to emphasise the intellectual faculty as a key element in God's service" (*The Gospel of Mark: A Commentary on the Greek text* [Eerdmans], 2002, p. 480).

Chapter Six

[1]King, *op. cit.*, p. 71.

[2]De Boer points out that "there are other writings which describe a struggle of the soul in the present" (citing specifically *The Exegesis of the Soul, Authoritative Teaching,* and the *Corpus Hermeticum* in a footnote) and points out that "it is difficult to decide whether the soul's struggle is a struggle in the present or a struggle after death" (*op. cit.*, p. 112).

[3]Cf. Schaberg, *op. cit.*, p. 174; Bourgeault, *Mary Magdalene,* p. 68.

[4]Bourgeault, *Mary Magdalene,* p. 65.

[5]King, *op. cit.*, p. 79.

[6]Cf. Tuckett, *op. cit.*, p. 185.

[7]William Johnston, ed., *The Cloud of Unknowing and the Book of Privy Counseling* (Image Books), 1973, p. 127.

[8]King, *op. cit.*, p. 79.

[9]For example, in his 1963 letter from a Birmingham jail, Dr. King listed "self-purification" as a necessary step prior to "direct action," and in his seminal work *Hind Swaraj,* Gandhi defined Indian "liberation" or "independence" *(swaraj)* by writing that "if

we become free, India is free. And in this thought you have a definition of Swaraj. It is Swaraj when we learn to rule ourselves. It is, therefore, in the palm of our hands. Do not consider this Swaraj to be like a dream. There is no idea of sitting still. The Swaraj that I wish to picture is such that, after we have once realized it, we shall endeavor to the end of our life-time to persuade others to do likewise. But such Swaraj has to be experienced, by each one for himself" (*The Collected Works of Mahatma Gandhi* [Electronic Book], New Delhi, Publications Division Government of India, 1999, vol. 10, p. 282).

Chapter Seven

[1]Marvin Meyer, with Esther A. De Boer, *The Gospels of Mary: The Secret Tradition of Mary Magdalene The Companion of Jesus* (HarperSanFrancisco), 2004, p. 68; cf. also Pistis Sophia 146.

[2]*Ibid.*

[3]Marvin Meyer, ed., *The Nag Hammadi Scriptures: The International Edition* (HarperOne), 2008, p. 153.

[4]*Ibid.,* p. 171.

[5]Cf. Tuckett, *op. cit.,* pp. 189,190.

[6]Cf. Schaberg, *op. cit.,* p. 180.

Chapter Eight

[1]Rev. Laura M. Grimes, Ph.D., *Sophia's Psalter,* p. 63.

[2]Johnston, *op. cit.,* p. 56.

Appendix

[1]For this and what follows, cf. De Boer, *op. cit.*, pp. 75,76,79; King, *The Gospel of Mary*, pp. 7-12.

[2]James M. Robinson, ed., *The Nag Hammadi Library in English* (Harper & Row), 1978. The Berlin Codex wasn't included among the codices discovered near Nag Hammadi, but two of the other four books in the Berlin Codex had turned up in that collection, which was discovered in 1945.

[3]The Papyrus Rylands 463, published in 1938, coincides with 17:5-19:5 of the Berlin Codex. The Papyrus Oxyrhynchus 3525, published in 1983, coincides with 9:5-10:13.

[4]Cf. Tuckett, *op. cit.*, pp. 9,10.

Bibliography

Barnstone, Willis, *The Restored New Testament: A New Translation with Commentary, Including the Gnostic Gospels Thomas, Mary, and Judas* (W.W. Norton & Company), 2009

Bauman, Lynn C., Bauman, Ward J., and Bourgeault, Cynthia, *The Luminous Gospels: Thomas, Mary Magdalene, and Philip* (Praxis Publishing), 2008

Bourgeault, Cynthia, *The Meaning of Mary Magdalene: Discovering the Woman at the Heart of Christianity* (Shambhala), 2010

Bourgeault, Cynthia, *The Wisdom Jesus: Transforming Heart and Mind – a New Perspective on Christ and His Message* (Shambhala), 2008

Bourgeault, Cynthia, *Centering Prayer and Inner Awakening* (Cowley Publications), 2004

Contemplative Outreach at:
http://www.contemplativeoutreach.org/

De Boer, Esther, *Mary Magdalene: Beyond the Myth* (Trinity Press International), 1997

France, R.T., *The Gospel of Mark: A Commentary on the Greek Text* (Eerdmans), 2002

Grimes, Laura M. *Sophia's Psalter*, 2011

Keating, Thomas, *Open Mind, Open Heart: The Contemplative Dimension of the Gospel* (Continuum), 2002

King, Karen L., *The Gospel of Mary of Magdala: Jesus and the First Woman Apostle* (Polebridge Press), 2003

Lambdin, Thomas O., *Introduction to Sahidic Coptic* (Mercer University Press), 1983

Layton, Bentley, *Coptic in 20 Lessons: Introduction to Sahidic Coptic With Exercises and Vocabularies* (Peeters), 2007

Leloup, Jean-Yves, *The Gospel of Mary Magdalene* (Inner Traditions), 2002

Leloup, Jean-Yves, *The Gospel of Philip: Jesus, Mary Magdalene, and the Gnosis of Sacred Union* (Inner Traditions), 2004

Leloup, Jean-Yves, *The Gospel of Thomas: The Gnostic Wisdom of Jesus* (Inner Traditions), 2005

McColman, Carl, *The Big Book of Christian Mysticism: The Essential Guide to Contemplative Spirituality* (Hampton Roads Publishing Company, Inc.), 2010

McGehee, Michael, "A Less Theological Reading of John 20:17," *Journal of Biblical Literature*, Vol. 105, No. 2

Meyer, Marvin, *The Gospel of Thomas: The Hidden Sayings of Jesus* (HarperSanFrancisco), 1992

Meyer, Marvin, with Esther A. De Boer, *The Gospels of Mary: The Secret Tradition of Mary Magdalene The Companion of Jesus* (HarperSanFrancisco), 2004

Meyer, Marvin, ed., *The Nag Hammadi Scriptures: The International Edition* (HarperOne), 2008

Miller, Robert J., *The Complete Gospels* (HarperSanFrancisco), 1994

Muyskens, J. David, *Forty Days to a Closer Walk with God: The Practice of Centering Prayer* (Upper Room Books), 2006

Muyskens, J. David, *Sacred Breath: 40 Days of Centering Prayer* (Upper Room Books), 2010

Pasquier, Anne, *L'Évangile Selon Marie* (Les Presses de l'Université Laval), 1983

Priests for Equality, *The Inclusive Bible: The First Egalitarian Translation* (Sheed & Ward), 2007

Robinson, James M., ed., *The Nag Hammadi Library in English* (Harper & Row), 1978

Schaberg, Jane, *The Resurrection of Mary Magdalene: Legends, Apocrypha, and the Christian Testament* (Continuum), 2004

Smith, Andrew Phillip *The Gospel of Philip: Annotated and Explained* (Skylight Paths Publishing), 2005

Starbird, Margaret, *The Woman with the Alabaster Jar: Mary Magdalene and the Holy Grail* (Bear & Company), 1993

The Collected Works of Mahatma Gandhi (Electronic Book), New Delhi, Publications Division Government of India, 1999, 98 volumes

Till, Walter C. and Schenke, Hans-Martin, *Die gnostischen Schriften des koptischen Papyrus Berolinensis* 8502 (Akademie Verlag), 1972

Tuckett, Christopher, *The Gospel of Mary* (Oxford University Press), 2007

Wilson, R. McL. and MacRae, George W., "The Gospel According to Mary," in *The Coptic Gnostic Library: A Complete Edition of the Nag Hammadi Codices, Vol. III*, ed. By James M. Robinson (Brill), 2000

Made in the USA
Columbia, SC
22 September 2023

23245079R00046